# No Shame

Hendrickson Books by Melissa Heiland

*A Mother's Comfort*
*La Esperanza de una Madre*

*A Mother's Journey*
*El Viaje de una Madre*

*You Are Wonderful*
*Eres Maravilloso*

*Get Set*

# No Shame

## A Devotional for Survivors of Sexual Abuse

**HENDRICKSON**
**PUBLISHERS**

*an imprint of Hendrickson Publishing Group*

**No Shame: A Devotional for Survivors of Sexual Abuse**

© 2023 Melissa Heiland

Published by Hendrickson Publishers
an imprint of Hendrickson Publishing Group
Hendrickson Publishers, LLC
P. O. Box 3473
Peabody, Massachusetts 01961-3473
www.hendricksonpublishinggroup.com

ISBN 978-1-4964-8208-2

*For more information, please contact:*

Melissa Heiland
www.beautifulfeetinternational.com

*Printed in the United States of America*

*First Printing — January 2023*

*This book is dedicated to you, the survivors.*
*You are seen. You are heard. You are loved.*

# Foreword

Dear Readers,

It is both shocking and heartbreaking to hear that, according to the Rape, Abuse & Incest National Network (RAINN), an American is sexually assaulted every 68 seconds.[1] Even more alarming is that this statistic would be even graver outside of the US, considering how much more taboo the subject is in other countries. You are likely holding this book for one of two reasons: you are a survivor of sexual assault or you wish to help a survivor. This book is certainly an invaluable tool in either endeavor. In the footnotes below, you will see just the beginnings of some resources for more information.

Sexual trauma holds the potential to fragment an individual's phenomenological experience.[2] That is, "normally integrated functions" of a person's body and mind become compartmentalized and separated.[3] The survivor experiences dissociation and confusion deep within the self. As Christians, we believe that there is not just the physical side to a person but also also a spiritual side—and that these two are related to each other in great degree. Forget to eat lunch and you

---

1. "About Sexual Assault," RAINN, https://www.rainn.org/about-sexual-assault.

2. Judith Lewis Herman, *Trauma and Recovery: The Aftermath of Violence from Domestic Abuse to Political Terror* (Boston: Basic Books, 2015).

3. Herman, *Trauma and Recovery*, 34.

may begin to act in ways you know are spiritually unhealthy, like losing your temper quickly or making an impulsive decision you later regret. The ramifications of sexual trauma, therefore, can certainly spill over into the spiritual side of life. And indeed, the goal throughout the journey to healing from any trauma—sexual included—is the recovered, reintegrated self.[4]

Such a journey for Christians, when they are ready, includes contemplation and engagement in the spiritual self. As Melissa Heiland gently reflects throughout this devotional, our understanding of God and God's stance toward us can be confusing or even painful in light of sexual assault. As a mental health therapist, I can say with a full heart that Melissa is a compassionate and paced guide as she considers Scripture, with its implications and applications, for the survivor of sexual abuse in small, succinct doses. This is a read that I believe is excellent to turn to not once, but many times. Survivors recover and reintegrate their internal self in the presence, promise, and protection of a God who, having walked the road from birth to public execution, knows all too well the journey of trauma and the redemption and resurrection possible in its wake.

This devotional is not in the place of counseling, and my recommendation of this book does not replace seeking the help of a mental health professional. Trauma of any kind, particularly of a sexual nature, most often requires a complex treatment course. This includes the help of a mental health

---

4. Heather Davediuk Gingrich and Fred C. Gingrich, *Treating Trauma in Christian Counseling* (Downers Grove, IL: IVP Academic, 2017).

professional, because trauma has a complex effect across multiple fronts of a person. This devotional should be viewed as an excellent supplemental tool in a robust therapeutic approach to helping the healing journey of survivors.

May God grant you the strength and peace needed with each step forward.

Lisa Clay
MACO, MANT
Gordon-Conwell Theological Seminary

# Acknowledgments

I would first like to thank the brave survivors who talked to me about their experiences, their feelings, their wounds, their healing. You are courageous, strong, and kind.

My sincere thanks to Paul Hendrickson of Hendrickson Publishing Group. Paul, your humility and grace continue to bless me. Thank you for answering God's call in your life and for your continued patience and kindness toward me.

Thank you, Lissi, for translating with love, tenderness, and sensitivity to the Holy Spirit.

Thank you to those who edited this work. I trust the Lord's leading as you worked.

I want to thank those who work with survivors to bring hope and healing. You are a blessing.

I am deeply grateful for each of my children: Michael, Josh, Melissa, Jack, Andy, and Nick. You are my inspiration and my joy.

I am also grateful for my grandchildren: Graciana, Matthew, Gabriel, Kara, Courtney, Anna, Carla, Madilyn, Jacob, and Eli. You fill this GiGi's life with love and laughter. May God protect you always.

Sincere thanks to my husband, Ken, who always encourages me to keep writing when my heart is full of self-doubt. Thank you for believing in God's call on my life and for the sacrifices you make when you allow me to answer his call.

My deepest gratitude is always for my Lord and Savior, Jesus Christ. He saved me, and he continues to hold me and heal me as I trust him in even the darkest of times.

# Dear Friend,

Survivors of abuse hear a lot of messages that condemn, confuse, and wound. These messages are based on lies. Truth is found in the word of God. I have spent two years asking the Lord to show me Scriptures to share with you that will bring you comfort and peace. I have written this for you at the prompting of the Holy Spirit so that you will know the truth and the truth will set you free.

With love,
Melissa

# DAY 1

## *Singing over You*

---

### Read Zephaniah 3:17

*The L<small>ORD</small> your God is with you,*
*the Mighty Warrior who saves.*
*He will take great delight in you;*
*in his love he will no longer rebuke you,*
*but will rejoice over you with singing.*

---

This verse is full of beautiful truths. Not only does God save you but he also *delights* in you. Take a moment and contemplate the magnitude of that statement. The God who created the whole world is singing over you. He takes delight in you. He loves you as a father. Not only is he a mighty warrior, but he is also gentle, like a parent singing over a child. Maybe you don't have any memories of a person singing to you. If so, then close your eyes now and imagine that display of love from God. What would he say? Would it be a song of encouragement? Hope?

Dear God, thank you for loving me and saving me. I have not always felt safe, and I am thankful to know that you are a mighty warrior who watches over me and delights in me. Please help me to find peace in your safety. Amen.

*How does it make you feel to think*
*about a God who loves you and rejoices*
*over you? Write your thoughts.*

2

# DAY 2

## Close to the Broken-Hearted

---

### Read Psalm 34:15–19

*The eyes of the L*ORD *are on the righteous,
and his ears are attentive to their cry;
but the face of the L*ORD *is against those who
do evil,
to blot out their name from the earth.
The righteous cry out, and the L*ORD *hears them;
he delivers them from all their troubles.
The L*ORD *is close to the brokenhearted
and saves those who are crushed in spirit.
The righteous person may have many troubles,
but the L*ORD *delivers him from them all.*

---

This passage brought me great comfort during a dark time in my life. I found comfort in the fact that God saw me and heard my cry. He promised to deliver me from what I was going through. I also found comfort in knowing that the Lord is just and that those who do evil will not go unpunished. The Lord will deliver the righteous from all their troubles.

> Dear God, thank you for seeing me and hearing me. Thank you for promising to deliver me from anything that I am going through. Help me to trust in your promises. Amen.

*How do you feel knowing that God sees and
hears you? Knowing that God is close to you,
listening to you, what do you want to tell him?*

# DAY 3

## A Strong Tower

### Read Proverbs 18:10

*The name of the Lord is a fortified tower;
the righteous run to it and are safe.*

Today we read that God is a fortress, a place of safety and protection. If you are like me, you may often feel afraid and exposed, unsure of whom you can trust. When we are afraid, we want to run and hide. God knows this and tells us to run to him instead. He knows our every fear and provides us with a fortified tower in his name. He always has our best interest at heart. It can be difficult to trust others after someone has betrayed us, but God will not do us harm. Run to God today and find a place of safety and rest.

Dear God, I thank you that I can run to you for safety. Please help me to remember that you offer healing when we come to you. Amen.

*Can you think of a place where you feel or
of a person who makes you feel safe? What
about this place or person makes you feel
safe? How can God provide safety for you?*

# DAY 4

## The Truth Will Set You Free

---

### Read John 8:32

*"Then you will know the truth, and
the truth will set you free."*

---

Many times, when someone abuses us, our our minds can get confused about what is true about ourselves. It can cause us to believe that we deserved what happened to us, that we are tainted and worthless. Abuse is rooted in deception and lies. Even though we might recognize the lies, they still affect us deeply. God tells us that we will know the truth and the truth will set us free. The truth is that the love of God is more powerful than anything that can ever happen to us. No matter what we have done and no matter what has been done to us, the blood of Christ covers it all. You are not defined by what happened to you. You are a person loved and valued by God.

God, I pray that you will show me the truth. Help me to see myself as you see me, a person deeply loved and cherished by you. Amen.

*What lies have you found yourself
believing? What is the truth?*

# DAY 5

## Familiar with Pain

---

### Read Isaiah 53:3

*He was despised and rejected by mankind,*
*a man of suffering, and familiar with pain.*
*Like one from whom people hide their faces*
*he was despised, and we held him in low esteem.*

---

There is often a seemingly unshakable sadness that comes after trauma. This persistent sadness has often made me feel defined by my suffering. This verse from Isaiah brings me great comfort because I remember that Jesus was called "a man of suffering." During Jesus' time on earth, he suffered betrayal from those close to him. He was rejected, mocked, and ultimately nailed to the cross, put to death for crimes he did not commit. He was innocent but still hated and scorned. He knows the pain of betrayal. He understands our suffering and pain. Jesus chose to suffer for our sakes because he valued our eternal salvation more than his life. He did not have to suffer, but did so in order that we could be free from the punishment for sin. His death on the cross paid the price for us so that we could have a relationship with God.

> Dear Jesus, thank you for suffering for me. Thank you for dying so that I could be forgiven. Let me remember your sacrifice when I start to feel defined by my suffering. Amen.

*Have you ever felt defined by your suffering?*
*Write out some words that you associate*
*with your identity. Do they match what*
*you want your identity to be?*

# DAY 6

## No Shame

---

### Read Isaiah 61:7

*Instead of your shame
      you will receive a double portion,
and instead of disgrace
      you will rejoice in your inheritance.
And so you will inherit a double portion in
      your land,
      and everlasting joy will be yours.*

---

For years, feelings of indescribable shame have washed over me and, in my mind, defined me. These feelings do not come from God. My prayer is that you will release these feelings of shame to the Lord. Your shame is based on the lie that you are responsible for what happened to you and that your trauma makes you unclean. You are not responsible. It is not your fault. God promises that he will remove your shame and replace it with everlasting joy. Will you receive this gift today?

Thank you, Father, for removing my shame. Thank you for your promise of a double portion and an inheritance with you. Amen.

*Which of God's promises do you
need to remember most?*

# DAY 7

## Well-Watered Garden

### Read Isaiah 58:11

*The LORD will guide you always;*
*he will satisfy your needs in a sun-scorched*
*land*
*and will strengthen your frame.*
*You will be like a well-watered garden,*
*like a spring whose waters never fail.*

Have you ever felt like you are lost in a desert, weak and thirsty? God knows, and he sees you. He will guide you and satisfy your needs. He will give you strength. Abuse zaps our strength, leaving us feeling weak, lost, and alone. God tells us that he will lift us up and give us all that we need. Although our life may feel like a desert, it will become a well-watered garden, bright with roses, lilies, sunflowers, and daisies. The flowers will flourish because the waters will never fail to flow. We may fail, but our Lord never does.

Thank you, Lord, for guiding me and strengthening me. Thank you that you never fail. Help me to rest in your promise of a well-watered garden after the sun-scorched desert. Amen.

*Imagine your life as a well-watered*
*garden. Describe or draw a picture of what*
*your new life in Jesus will look like.*

# DAY 8

## Everlasting Life

---

### Read John 3:16

*"For God so loved the world that he gave his one and only Son, that whoever believes in him shall not perish but have eternal life."*

---

Since the beginning, God has loved us. The Bible teaches us that we are all separated from God because he is perfect and we are not. God knew that we would choose something other than him that would lead us to separation and destruction. But because God loves us, he does not want this separation. He made a way for us to be forgiven from our sins and live with him forever, both while we are here on earth and after we die. God sent his Son, Jesus, to die on a cross, taking the punishment for our sin upon himself. Jesus was perfect, and so our sins were perfectly cleansed through his sacrifice. He did not deserve to die, but rather chose to die so that we could live. On the third day after his death, he rose from the dead and ascended to heaven. When we trust and believe that Jesus died for us and rose again, we will be saved.

> Dear God, I know that I have made mistakes and that I need forgiveness. I believe that Jesus died on the cross for me and rose again. I trust Jesus to save me. Amen.

*Have you trusted Jesus as your Savior? Would you trust him today? Write your own prayer to God.*

# DAY 9

## *Full Life*

---

### Read John 10:10

*"The thief comes only to steal and kill and destroy; I have come that they may have life, and have it to the full."*

---

Abusers are like thieves. They steal something from us. It might be your safety, your peace, your trust, or even a period of time in your life that belonged to you. They do not have your well-being in mind. Often, they are people close to us, which makes the pain even greater. But John 10:10 tells us that Jesus came so that we could have life. Our lives do not have to be centered around the destruction that our abusers caused. God has made a way for us to have abundant, joy-filled lives. Regardless of what we have experienced in the past, we are far more than what a thief stole from us. God has given us a new life—a better life—and one that is far greater than we can imagine.

> Dear God, thank you for your good gifts. I know that in you, I have a new life. Help me to live my life to the full. In Jesus' name, amen.

*What does a joy-filled life look like to you? What are some things you can do that will help you experience joy?*

# DAY 10

## Tears in a Bottle

---

### Read Psalm 56:8

*You keep track of all my sorrows.*
*You have collected all my tears in your bottle.*
*You have recorded each one in your book. (NLT)*

---

I have loved this verse since I was a child. My life, like yours, has been filled with pain. The thought of a loving Father in heaven who collects all my tears is overwhelming. I imagine that God's bottle for us is enormous. Every tear that we have cried silently or screamed aloud is held by our Father in heaven. He sees us, loves us, and never forgets us. He writes every sorrow in his book and collects each tear. You, my friend, are seen and cherished.

> Thank you, God, for hearing my cries, even when they were silent ones. I cannot imagine how vast your love is for me, that you would collect every tear. Thank you for the care you have for each of them. Amen.

*Draw a picture of a bottle. Write words*
*inside the bottle that represent your pain*
*and tears. Remember that God sees all*
*of them and cares about them.*

# DAY 11

## God's Wrath

### Read Romans 12:19

*Do not take revenge, my dear friends, but leave room for God's wrath, for it is written: "It is mine to avenge; I will repay," says the Lord.*

I have often thought about revenge. I have wanted to hurt the person who caused so much pain in my life. This has been a real struggle for me, an+d maybe it has been for you too. God knows everything about us, including how we want revenge on the people who hurt us terribly. He also knows that getting revenge will not bring us peace. He calls us "dear friends" when he encourages us not to take revenge on those who have hurt us. His heart is full of compassion for us. And so, for our own good, he promises that he will repay those who have hurt us. He assures us that he is angry with them and that their deeds will not go unpunished. The burden of justice is not on our shoulders.

Dear God, I thank you that you love me and protect me by promising to repay those who have hurt me. Help me to trust in the peace that you promise me. Amen.

*How do you feel knowing that it is not up to you to repay evil for evil? Do you struggle with that truth?*

# DAY 12

## God's Plan for You

---

### Read Jeremiah 29:11–13

*For I know the plans I have for you," declares the L*ORD*, "plans to prosper you and not to harm you, plans to give you hope and a future. Then you will call on me and come and pray to me, and I will listen to you. You will seek me and find me when you seek me with all your heart."*

---

God has a plan for your life, and it is good. Your hopelessness in the present does not change God's promise of a plan for you to prosper, to give you hope for a future. God's word states that his plans are not to harm you. He has had great plans for you since the beginning. If you call on the Lord's name and pray to him, he will listen to you. And if you seek him with all your heart, you will find him. But do not neglect your part. Take some time to talk to him now.

> Dear God, I know that you are good. Thank you for giving me hope for the future. Thank you for listening to me when I pray and making yourself known to me. Amen.

*What are some dreams you have for the future? Use this space to write your dreams.*

# DAY 13

## Engraved on His Hand

---

### Read Isaiah 49:16

*See, I have engraved you on the palms of my
hands;
your walls are ever before me.*

---

Have you ever felt invisible, like no one could see you? Sometimes our pain is so great that we need support from other people, but no one seems to notice or care. The Bible tells us that God has engraved us on the palm of his hand. He is always thinking of us. There is never a moment where you and I are not on God's mind. His eyes are always on us. We are seen and loved. We can cry out to God, and he will hear us and comfort us.

Father, it is overwhelming to think about being engraved on the palm of your hand. Thank you for loving me so much. Help me to feel your love and to remember how much you love me. Amen.

*Draw a picture of a hand and write your name
on the hand. Write about what it means to you
to be engraved on the palm of God's hand.*

# DAY 14

## Rivers in the Desert

**Read Isaiah 43:19**

*Behold, I am doing a new thing;*
*now it springs forth, do you not perceive it?*
*I will make a way in the wilderness*
*and rivers in the desert. (ESV)*

Sometimes we may feel as if we are in the wilderness—lost without hope or dying of thirst in the desert. But this verse tells us that God is doing something new. Our God is a God of miracles. He will make a way in the wilderness and create rivers in our desert. God asks us, "Do you not perceive it?" Do you feel hope rising in you? He is doing something new and great in your life. He is making a way for you, bringing you new life and hope.

Thank you, God, for being a God of miracles. Thank you for giving me hope and doing something new in my life. I want to let go of the hurt of the past and find joy in the future. Amen.

*Draw a picture that represents your wilderness*
*or desert experience. What do you think is*
*the new thing God is doing in your life?*

# DAY 15

## Yesterday, Today, and Forever

---

### Read Hebrews 13:8

*Jesus Christ is the same yesterday and today and forever.*

---

People can be frightening at times. There are those who say they love us and still intentionally hurt us. Some days they are kind, and some days they are cruel. This leaves us feeling disoriented, confused, and afraid of saying or doing something to provoke them.

But God is reliable and unchanging. He is the same yesterday, today, and forever. Know that he is always on our side and can be trusted in all things. We are safe and secure in Jesus.

Jesus, I thank you that you are unchanging and can be trusted in all things. Help me to rest in you as I learn to trust you more. Amen.

*Make a list of things that make you feel safe. It could include people, places, songs, Bible verses, or other things.*

# DAY 16

## *God of Peace*

---

### Read 1 Corinthians 14:33

*For God is not a God of disorder but of peace—as in all the congregations of the Lord's people.*

---

When someone is hurting us, we often feel confused. Even after the abuse has ended, the confusion often remains. We feel confused about ourselves, our identity, our value, our place in the world. We are confused about why we suffered, why it happened to us. The Bible tells us that God is not a God of disorder, but a God of peace. It is normal to have questions, and it is healthy to talk with someone you trust about your suffering. Ultimately, God will give you peace. I encourage you to read his word each day and let his truths heal you and bring you peace.

Father, I thank you that you are a God of peace. Remove confusion from my mind. Help me to feel peace in my heart. Help me to see myself through your eyes. Amen.

*Tell the Lord what confuses you and ask him to replace your confusion with his peace.*

# DAY 17

## The Lord Receives Me

---

### Read Psalm 27:10

*Though my father and mother forsake me,
the L*ORD *will receive me.*

You may have been abused by a parent. Or perhaps a parent knew about it and didn't protect you or didn't believe you. Maybe you were rejected by a parent as a result of the abuse. If any of these things has happened to you, I am so sorry. That was not God's plan for you. Parents are supposed to love, nurture, and protect their children. God promises that if your parents failed to care for you, you are not alone. The Lord himself will receive you and honor you as his child. He is the perfect parent who loves you with his endless love.

Father, people have let me down so much in my life. You know my pain. Thank you for always being there for me and promising to never leave me. Amen.

*What is our inheritance as children of
God? What does God offer to us now?*

# DAY 18

## No More Tears

---

### Read Revelation 21:4

*He will wipe every tear from their eyes. There will
be no more death or mourning or crying or pain,
for the old order of things has passed away.*

---

I love to read about heaven. We know that there is pain and
suffering on earth, but God promises heaven to those who
trust Jesus as their savior. In heaven there is no crying, no
pain. The Lord gives us comfort here on earth and something
even more wonderful in heaven. In heaven, our hearts will be
made whole. Nothing will ever hurt us again. The old order
of things will have passed away and the new will have come.
I have such joy as I think about this.

> Dear God, thank you for sending Jesus to die for us so that
> we can live forever with you in heaven. Thank you that you
> will wipe every tear from our eyes. In Jesus' name, amen.

*What do you look forward to in heaven? Describe
or draw a picture of what you imagine it to be.*

# DAY 19

## Help from the Lord

---

### Read Psalm 121:1–2

*I lift up my eyes to the mountains—*
*where does my help come from?*
*My help comes from the LORD,*
*the Maker of heaven and earth.*

Do you feel helpless? Do you ever feel like the pain is too much for you to handle alone? God is ready to help you. As I write, I am looking out at the ocean that God created. It is vast and fierce and wild. Our powerful God created the oceans and the mountains, things that are so much steadier and more long-lasting than our worries. He is so much more powerful than even these. Do not doubt that he will save you from every trouble. He can deliver you from any circumstance.

> Thank you, Lord, for helping me. I see your strength in the creation around me. I know you will help me. Amen.

*What kind of help do you need? Tell the*
*Lord and trust him to provide it.*

# DAY 20

## The Love of Christ

### Read Ephesians 3:16–18

*I pray that out of his glorious riches he may strengthen you with power through his Spirit in your inner being, so that Christ may dwell in your hearts through faith. And I pray that you, being rooted and established in love, may have power, together with all the Lord's holy people, to grasp how wide and long and high and deep is the love of Christ.*

God's love for you is enormous. Sometimes it can be hard to receive love when you have been hurt. You might even feel unworthy or incapable of receiving love. God wants you to grasp how wide and high and deep his love for you is. His love knows no bounds. Out of his glorious riches, he strengthens us so that Christ can dwell in our hearts. Rooted in him, you will see how great his love is for you. Pray that you will receive that power as Christ dwells in your heart.

Thank you, God, for the depths of your love. Help me to receive Christ and understand just how vast your love for me is. In Jesus' name, amen.

*How have you felt God's love? Make a list of the ways God has shown you his love in your life.*

# DAY 21

## Committed No Sin

---

### Read Deuteronomy 22:25-26

*But if out in the country a man happens to meet a young woman pledged to be married and rapes her, only the man who has done this shall die. Do nothing to the woman; she has committed no sin deserving death. This case is like that of someone who attacks and murders a neighbor.*

---

The Old Testament contains many rules and laws. I am including this law to remind you of something important. People who abuse others are never coerced into doing so. The Bible says they are like someone who attacks and murders a neighbor. Other people may judge you and you might even blame yourself, but these things are all lies and confusion that come from the enemy. You are in no way responsible for the crimes committed against you. When these thoughts come to your mind, recognize that they are lies and speak truth to yourself. It is not your fault.

> Dear God, thank you for showing me that what happened to me is not my fault. Help me to recognize lies when I hear them from others and myself. Help me to believe truth. In Jesus' name, amen.

*Do you still carry the guilt of another person's sin? Pray that God will release that burden from you.*

# DAY 22

## *How Long, Lord?*

---

### Read Psalm 6:2-4

*Have mercy on me, Lord, for I am faint;*
*heal me, Lord, for my bones are in agony.*
*My soul is in deep anguish.*
*How long, Lord, how long?*
*Turn, Lord, and deliver me;*
*save me because of your unfailing love.*

---

The pain from sexual abuse lasts a long time. In these verses, we see the phrases "deep aguish" and "agony." The writer is faint and cries out to the Lord, "How long?" You may have experienced these feelings of unending pain and longed for relief. It may seem that there is nothing you can do to escape the residual pain that your assault has left on you. It might seem impossible to fully recover from whatever wrong has been done to you. But when we are feeling faint, the psalmist writes words of renewal: *mercy, heal, deliver, save.* The Lord sees your pain and will deliver you. Cry out to him for healing, and he will have mercy on you and save you.

Thank you, Lord, for seeing my pain. I beg you to heal me, deliver me, save me. Comfort me when it seems as though my suffering will last forever. Amen.

*On one half of the page write words that describe your pain. On the other half, write words that describe God (for example: kind, strong, merciful).*

# DAY 23

## Refuge

---

### Read Psalm 91:4

*He will cover you with his feathers,*
*and under his wings you will find refuge;*
*his faithfulness will be your shield and rampart.*

---

"Refuge" is defined as shelter or protection from danger or distress. We usually think of a strong fortress or castle wall that will keep evil away from us. However, this psalm describes God's love like that of a caring mother bird who shelters her young under her wings. Under his wings, we have refuge. He will cover us and protect us. His faithfulness shields us from danger. His faithfulness with be our protection from harm.

> Father, thank you for covering me with your wings. Thank you for your faithfulness, which you promise will protect me. Amen.

> *What does the image of God as mother*
> *evoke? How does that shape the way*
> *that you consider God's protection?*

# DAY 24

## The Love of God

---

### Read Romans 8:38–39

*I am convinced that neither death nor life, neither angels nor demons, neither the present nor the future, nor any powers, neither height nor depth, nor anything else in all creation, will be able to separate us from the love of God that is in Christ Jesus our Lord.*

---

The concept of love can be confusing. People say they love us and yet they hurt us. Sometimes they walk away. Love is known to bring both joy and pain. God's love is different. God's love is unending and boundless. It is perfect and never fails. God's love for us is more powerful than we can imagine. It is so powerful that nothing in all creation, even time itself, can separate us from the love of God in Christ Jesus.

> Thank you, God, for loving me. Knowing that nothing can separate me from your love gives me assurance in your presence. Amen.

*What is something that has made you feel separated from God? What do you know now about his promises?*

# DAY 25

## Head Lifted High

---

### Read Psalm 3:3

*But you, LORD, are a shield around me,*
*my glory, the One who lifts my head high.*

---

I love this verse. Sorrow, shame, and pain can cause us to go through life downcast, looking at the ground. When our confidence is shattered, it is hard to view ourselves as worth more than our suffering. We are afraid to look up and meet people's eyes as equals. But with God, we can lift our heads up high. He tells us not to be ashamed or afraid. He is our shield and our protector. We have nothing to fear.

Thank you, God, for lifting my head. I find my courage in you. Thank you for shielding me. Amen.

*Have you ever had your confidence shattered? Think about God shielding you and lifting your head.*

# DAY 26

## You Are Mine

---

### Read Isaiah 43:1

*But now, this is what the L*ord *says—*
*he who created you, Jacob,*
*he who formed you, Israel:*
*"Do not fear, for I have redeemed you;*
*I have summoned you by name; you are mine."*

---

God created and formed you with intention. How wonderful it is that God summons you by name! You will face trials, but you will never face them alone. God is with you and loves you with an everlasting love. You do not have to be afraid. God is holding you tightly and will never let you go. When you feel like the waters of life will drown you, cling to him.

> Father, thank you that even when I feel like I can't hold on, you are holding me, keeping me safe. Thank you for calling me by name. Amen.

> *Imagine Jesus calling your name, holding*
> *you, protecting you. What do you fear?*
> *How does knowing that Jesus is carrying*
> *you help you to face your fears?*

# DAY 27

## *Without Cost*

---

### Read Isaiah 55:1–2

*Come, all you who are thirsty,*
*come to the waters;*
*and you who have no money,*
*come, buy and eat!*
*Come, buy wine and milk*
*without money and without cost.*
*Why spend money on what is not bread,*
*and your labor on what does not satisfy?*
*Listen, listen to me, and eat what is good,*
*and you will delight in the richest of fare.*

---

Many times, we experience love that is conditional. Someone loves us only when we do what they expect from us. As soon as we do not comply with their wishes, we are cast aside. Love from them comes with a cost, but the love we receive from God is unconditional. He will never stop loving us. When we have nothing to offer the Lord, he gives to us freely. We do not have to earn his love. However, he tells us not to labor for food that will not satisfy—conditional love that will hurt us. Come to God for love that will never fail.

Father, thank you for loving me. Help me to see the kind of love that is pure and unconditional. Help me to choose that love every time. Amen.

*What kind of love has failed you before? What*
*does unconditional love mean to you?*

# DAY 28

## Heart of Stone

---

### Read Ezekiel 36:26

*I will give you a new heart and put a new
spirit in you; I will remove from you your heart
of stone and give you a heart of flesh.*

---

Suffering can cause our hearts to turn cold. We stop feeling
and caring because our hearts and minds are overloaded. We
simply cannot take any more. We shut down. Shutting down
in the face of danger is a defense mechanism designed for
our protection. However, it is sometimes difficult to let down
our defenses. No one wants to live with a heart of stone, but
sometimes it seems there is no way out. God says he will give
us a new heart and a new spirit. He takes our heart of stone
and replaces it with a heart of flesh. When we receive the love
of God, we learn to love and trust, regardless of our past. The
love of Jesus makes all things new.

Thank you, Lord, for allowing me to put down my defenses
and heal from past hurt. Help me to trust your love for me.
Amen.

*What parts of your heart feel as if they are
made of stone? Ask God to remove your heart
of stone and give you a heart of flesh.*

# DAY 29

## You Are Clean

---

### Read John 15:3

*"You are already clean because of the
word I have spoken to you."*

---

You are clean. Have you ever felt the gravity of that statement? The things some people do to us can make us feel dirty and tainted. We want to scrub it straight from our skin, and yet the feeling of being filthy never goes away. We can't scrub hard enough. But God says that we are *already* clean because of the word he has spoken to us. When you become a child of God through faith in Jesus, you are declared clean. You are clean, and nothing that anyone does to you will ever change that.

> Thank you, Father, that I am clean. Help me to remember these words you have spoken to me and truly believe them. In Jesus' name, amen.

*Have you ever felt that there is nothing you can do to be made whole again? What does it mean to you when you hear that God says you are clean?*

# DAY 30

## *Compassion*

---

### Read Isaiah 51:3

*The LORD will surely comfort Zion*
*and will look with compassion on all her ruins;*
*he will make her deserts like Eden,*
*her wastelands like the garden of the LORD.*
*Joy and gladness will be found in her,*
*thanksgiving and the sound of singing.*

---

Jesus looks with compassion at the ruins of our lives. He will make our deserts become like the Garden of Eden, our wastelands like paradise. He will restore what has been stripped away. Note the imagery of growth and life in this verse. When you come to believe that you have nothing left in yourself to sustain life, God grows a beautiful garden. In that restoration, you will sing and be joyful. God will give us hearts full of thanksgiving and rejoicing. His love washes over us, cleansing us, restoring us, giving us hope for the future.

> Father, help me to see myself through your eyes. Thank you for your comfort and compassion. Thank you for making me sing. Amen.

*Write lyrics of thanksgiving and praise to*
*God for all he has done in your life.*

# DAY 31

## Without Shame

---

### Read Psalm 34:4–5

*I sought the L*ORD*, and he answered me;*
*he delivered me from all my fears.*
*Those who look to him are radiant;*
*their faces are never covered with shame.*

---

The Lord promises that when we look for him, we will find him. When we search for him and rely on him, he delivers us from all our fears. On the mountain of Sinai, Moses spoke with the Lord and returned to the people of Israel with his face radiant like the sun. This psalm speaks of our own faces when we look to God. We are like Moses coming down from Mount Sinai. When we look to God, our faces shine with his presence. We are free from shame.

Thank you, Lord, for erasing my shame and answering my call. Help me to keep my eyes on you.

*Focus your heart and mind on the Lord. Imagine*
*that your face is radiant, as God's word says.*
*How would that confidence affect you?*

# DAY 32

## Blameless

### Read Ephesians 1:3-5

*Praise be to the God and Father of our Lord Jesus Christ, who has blessed us in the heavenly realms with every spiritual blessing in Christ. For he chose us in him before the creation of the world to be holy and blameless in his sight. In love he predestined us for adoption to sonship through Jesus Christ, in accordance with his pleasure and will.*

The Bible tells us that God chose us before the beginning of the world to be holy and blameless in his sight. We were not only chosen for salvation; we were chosen as children of Christ! Through his sacrifice of love, Jesus died on the cross to take the punishment for our sin so that we can live eternally as his children. When we trust Jesus as our savior, all sin is erased. God forgives us completely. He does not see our sin; only the blood of Christ making us clean. Not only are we blessed here and now, but we are also blessed in the heavenly realms with every spiritual blessing in Christ. We are his sons and daughters, chosen from the beginning of time to be loved by God.

Thank you, Lord, for choosing me. Thank you for the promise of an eternity of blessings. In Jesus' name, amen.

*How do you feel knowing that God choose you before he created the world? What does it mean to be adopted as God's child?*

# DAY 33

## *Peace*

---

### Read John 14:27

*"Peace I leave with you; my peace I give you. I do not give to you as the world gives. Do not let your hearts be troubled and do not be afraid."*

---

Our hearts can be quite troubled, sometimes making it difficult for us to eat, sleep, or concentrate. We replay hurtful scenarios again and again in our minds. We cannot find rest. But God gives us peace. It comes from his heart to ours, allowing us to rest amid the storms of life. He tells us not to let our hearts be troubled. We need not fear. He does not give to us as the world gives: something fleeting that is bought with a price. God's peace is real and lasting. He is with us and cares for us.

> Father, thank you for giving me your peace. Help me to be free from the fear that keeps me from rest. In Jesus' name, amen.

*When you think of peace, what picture comes to mind? What steals your peace?*

# DAY 34

## Rebuilt

---

### Read Jeremiah 31:3-5

*The L*ORD *appeared to us in the past, saying:*

*"I have loved you with an everlasting love;*
*I have drawn you with unfailing kindness.*
*I will build you up again,*
*and you, Virgin Israel, will be rebuilt.*
*Again you will take up your timbrels*
*and go out to dance with the joyful.*
*Again you will plant vineyards*
*on the hills of Samaria;*
*the farmers will plant them*
*and enjoy their fruit."*

---

Abuse tears us down, but God rebuilds. This passage describes God rebuilding joy and hope in our lives through his everlasting love. Because of his love and kindness, we will dance and sing with joy. We will have fruitful, meaningful lives as we receive his love. What was taken will be restored. We will have joy and purpose, and we will praise him.

Thank you, God, for building me up, for restoring hope and peace in my life. Amen.

*What is something that you want*
*God to rebuild in your life?*

# DAY 35

## Healed

### Read Matthew 9:20–22

*A woman who had been subject to bleeding
for twelve years came up behind [Jesus] and
touched the edge of his cloak. She said to herself,
"If I only touch his cloak, I will be healed."
Jesus turned and saw her. "Take heart, daughter,"
he said, "your faith has healed you." And the
woman was healed at that moment.*

This story tells of a woman who had been sick for twelve years. She believed that if she could just touch the hem of Jesus' clothes, she would be healed. She had barely touched him, yet she was healed because of her faith.

We have wounds that Jesus can heal as well. Trust him to heal your heart today.

Father, thank you, for building my faith with your word, the Bible. Heal me from the wounds of my past. I trust you. Amen.

*How do you think the woman in this story felt when
she was healed? Has the Lord healed you from past
hurts? Thank him for what he has done for you
and ask him to heal any wounds that remain.*

# DAY 36

## Door of Hope

---

### Read Hosea 2:14–15

*Therefore I am now going to allure her;*
*I will lead her into the wilderness*
*and speak tenderly to her.*
*There I will give her back her vineyards,*
*and will make the Valley of Achor a door*
*of hope.*
*There she will respond as in the days of her youth,*
*as in the day she came up out of Egypt.*

---

When we are feeling lost, Jesus speaks tenderly to us in the wilderness of our lives. It is easy to feel trapped in that endless desert, where there seems to be nothing good. We see no way out. Then, unexpectedly, God shows us a door of hope. There is a place for us on the other side of pain. In the desert, God blesses us with vineyards so that we will trust in him. He will provide.

O God, I thank you for giving me hope, for restoring my trust in you. I sing praises to you.

*As you think about your future,*
*what gives you joy?*

# DAY 37

## Confidence

---

### Read Hebrews 13:6

*So we say with confidence,*

*"The Lord is my helper; I will not be afraid.*
*What can mere mortals do to me?"*

---

When people hurt us, use us, and deceive us, it strips us of our confidence. It closes our mouths. We live in fear of what will happen to us and what people will say about us. God changes all of that. He is our helper in our times of trouble. We can speak with confidence, knowing that God is on our side. There is nothing that any person can do to us to separate us from the love of God. There is nothing too powerful for him. We no longer have to be intimidated by those who want to control us. The Lord is our protector and helper.

Thank you, God, for protecting me. Help me remember that I no longer need to fear people because you are my helper.

*Who have you feared in the past? How does knowing that God is helping you give you confidence and alleviate your fears?*

# DAY 38

## A New Creation

---

### Read 2 Corinthians 5:17

*If anyone is in Christ, he is a new creation. The old has passed away; behold, the new has come.*

---

There are many things that are painful to remember but impossible to forget. Too often, we get stuck in an unhealthy mentality that our lives revolve around our trauma. It prevents us from being able to grow through our hardships. But God gives us a beautiful promise in this verse. He tells us that once we trust Jesus, the old self is gone. He makes us a new creation, whole and complete in him. We no longer have to live in our suffering or worry about the past. We are new and whole in Christ.

> Thank you, God, for making me a new creation in Jesus. It is comforting to know that the old has gone and the new is here! Amen.

*What does it mean to you to be a new creation?*
*What does that mean for your journey of healing?*

# DAY 39

## *Delivered*

---

### Read Psalm 34:7

*The angel of the L*ORD *encamps around those
who fear him,
and he delivers them.*

---

Repeatedly, God tells us we do not have to be afraid. Throughout the Bible, he proves that he is with his people through every danger. He protected the Israelites as they wandered in the wilderness, fought with neighboring nations, and even found themselves in captivity because they rejected God. He also protected individuals—Elijah, Daniel, Ruth, and Esther, to name a few. God is surrounding us, delivering us from all evil. We can be sure of his love. He will never let us down.

> Thank you, God, for surrounding me with your love and protection. Thank you for delivering me when I need your help. In Jesus' name, amen.

*Draw a picture of yourself surrounded by
God's love and protection. Write a prayer of
thanksgiving to God for delivering you.*

# DAY 40

## The Peace of God

---

### Read Philippians 4:6-7

*Do not be anxious about anything, but in every situation, by prayer and petition, with thanksgiving, present your requests to God. And the peace of God, which transcends all understanding, will guard your hearts and your minds in Christ Jesus.*

---

We all want peace, but it seems impossible to attain. The news is full of wars in politics and wars between nations. We even war within ourselves, fretting endlessly about things that are beyond our control. But God gives peace that transcends all understanding, even for inexplicable anxiety. If we ask for peace, God will grant it. His peace is not the same as ours. The peace of God will guard our hearts and minds in Christ Jesus.

> God, how I long for your peace. Help me to bring everything to you in prayer, trusting you. Thank you for hearing my cries and answering me. In Jesus' name, amen.

*Tell God the things that are troubling you. Ask him to give you his peace.*